PHANTOM HUE

Phantom Hue

Schyler Butler

CavanKerry
PRESS

For more information, write to Permissions, CavanKerry Press, 5 Horizon Road #2403, Fort Lee, New Jersey 07024.

CavanKerry Press Ltd.
Fort Lee, New Jersey
www.cavankerrypress.org

Publisher's Cataloging-in-Publication Data
provided by Five Rainbows Cataloging Services

Names: Butler, Schyler, author. | Ayers, Sayuri, writer of foreward.
Title: Phantom Hue / Schyler Butler.
Description: Fort Lee, NJ : CavanKerry Press, 2026.
Identifiers: ISBN 978-1-960327-22-2 (paperback)
Subjects: LCSH: Poetry. | Race relations--Poetry. | Spirituality--Poetry. | Generational trauma--Poetry. | White supremacy movements--Poetry. | Poetry--Women authors. | African American women--Poetry. | BISAC: POETRY / African American & Black. | POETRY / Women Authors. | POETRY / Subjects & Themes / Diversity & Multicultural.
Classification: LCC PS3557.I55 B98 P43 (print) | DDC 811.6--dc23.

Cover artwork: "Ruth's Easter Pageant" by Tiffany Lawson
Cover design by Gabriel Cleveland and Natasha Kane
Interior design by Natasha Kane
First Edition 2026, Printed in the United States of America

EMERGING VOICES
CAVANKERRY
PRESS

CavanKerry Press is dedicated to springboarding the careers of previously unpublished, early, and midcareer poets with our Emerging Voices series.

NEW JERSEY STATE COUNCIL ON THE ARTS EST. 1966

Made possible by funds from the New Jersey State Council on the Arts, a partner agency of the National Endowment for the Arts.

discover jersey arts

NATIONAL ENDOWMENT for the ARTS
arts.gov

CavanKerry Press is grateful for the generous support it receives from the New Jersey State Council on the Arts, as well as the following funders:

The Academy of American Poets
Bergen County Arts
Community of Literary Magazines and Presses
National Book Foundation
New Jersey Arts and Culture Renewal Fund
New Jersey Council for the Humanities
New Jersey Cultural Trust
New Jersey Economic Development Authority
The Poetry Foundation

Contents

Foreword

In 1999, I sat cross-legged on a tatami in my dorm room in Osaka, Japan. I traced the sun-scented grasses of the mat, while *Birth of the Cool* streamed through the CD player. The moon's glow dimmed under the glare of the city's neon lights.

This was the first time I was immersed in my father's culture, where I walked the streets of Hirakata alongside women whose faces mirrored mine. It was also the year that I was entrenched in an abusive relationship with a White man. I wavered between terror and infatuation, unwilling to break free of his oppression.

After this brush with violence, I became even more fearful and clung to the lie that I was powerless and worthless. As a result, I continued to capitulate to White supremacy. Instead of treasuring my Chinese and Japanese heritage, I concealed my otherness from my White friends. I exchanged large portions of my spirit for scraps of acceptance and approval. My identity warped and faded as I knelt in the searing White light.

I look back at that young woman with sadness and compassion. At the time, she was convinced that peace and safety were worth the loss of herself. She believed that she deserved to become mist, a ghost. For years, I did not have words to describe my tragic self-erasure. But now, Schyler Butler's *Phantom Hue* provides me with this language.

Truth exposes the darkest parts of ourselves. Butler's poems wound me with their sharp clarity, revealing my toxic desire for Whiteness. She confronts the reasons why women like myself are drawn to Whiteness. In "Postcolonial Triumph," Butler describes how BIPOC women are forced to assimilate into White culture as a form of survival:

I want to be White
meaning
I want to be human
meaning
I want to be free
meaning
I want to live

For me, "Postcolonial Triumph" serves as both truth and warning, highlighting the irony of self-preservation through self-erasure.

Throughout *Phantom Hue,* Butler continues to confront the harmful entanglement of women of color with Whiteness. With deft, sharply honed language, Butler unmasks Whiteness that poses as a protector and provider, revealing its brutal machinery that ultimately maims. "Dream Dialogue Where I Recount the Rape of My Father's Great Oma, 1896," "A Neighbor Tells What Happened to My Father's Aunt in Chillicothe, 1983," and "Bonnaroo, 2012" demonstrate how White supremacy intrudes on the lives of Black women with a violence that snakes through American history.

As Butler disrupts the narrative of salvation through Whiteness, she illuminates a new path toward emancipation. Butler weaves family experience with history to create a full-throated declaration of freedom through resistance. Butler forges these moments of Black brilliance through poems like "First Run" and "Dream of Clintonville After We All Move In," where "every old Chevy thumps the heavy nectar of our rap" and "the streets are not littered with bones . . . allowing a child to lead them through a ravine so baffling with joy."

As importantly, *Phantom Hue* is the prophetic, luminous voice of a Black artist. In "Intersectional Guillotine," Butler asserts:

what is my art if not the question—
what is my responsibility—
what is yours—

Butler's challenge cleaves my spirit, freeing me from the portion that longs for Whiteness and its conditional promises of protection and provision. She severs the connection between survival and assimilation and offers a way to thrive and resist, even under oppression. Her poems call for me to cease pouring into the broken vessel of Whiteness, urging me to instead drink deeply from ancestral rivers of knowledge and wisdom and to create art that shatters and reveals.

Phantom Hue is the gleaming implement of truth with the power to excise metastasizing lies. To me, the girl and woman, and to you, the reader, Butler offers this beautiful blade. We must make the decision to remain in its light, to yield to its wounding and healing.

—Sayuri Matsuura Ayers, MA, MFA
author of *The Woman, The River*
Columbus, Ohio
April 2026

And if it hurt—pulling asunder what their grandfathers had put together—it was nothing compared to what they had endured and what they might become if they did not begin anew.

—Toni Morrison, *Paradise*

I

Bravata

Mama, push up your cleavage till they burst
above that size-too-small V-neck. Tuck
your stomach fat down the waistband of your
high-rise skinnies. Turn around and watch
your behind pop the glass of your cheap floor
length. Don't matter you thirty-five with three
kids; don't matter us girls are watching.
Mama, you got a body: Demand the world see.
Ain't that the least it can do after giving you
philanderer after philanderer, their lips hope
saturated then licked dry after tasting beneath
your miniskirt, beneath the plunging lace and
deep cuts of your sight-curdling bravata, you
wearing the same stilettos your mama wore.
Mama, don't cry now; us children are watching.

Star-Crossed

the inhabitants of Earth
cried out, lifting their arms
to catch the strange, familiar bodies.

—Tim Seibles
"Welcome Home"

Only you read me Seibles on the first date,
you with fresh twists and eyes
like event horizons, my story
a mirror on the border of your light.
You take one look and download the image:
My bare leg extended on any street that will have me
until the right White man comes.
"Welcome Home" complements the candlelit beige
of futon no more used than a lighter,
and in between verses we delegate vocal spasms
on how similar our past, your lips mouthing
the knotted threads that indicate how often
and how hard we both tried
to love the children of our oppressors.
Not even we knew how inevitable the first kiss.

Variants of the Same Story, II

Imagine an iris plucked
because she looks nothing like her mother.
Imagine her womb as portal
where a man's children
may multiply generations that claim
what he could not.
Imagine a body the incantation
honoring the dominance of white.
Imagine the man, half a millennium bound
to his color, slashed unholy like arsenic.
Imagine he plucks the flower
like she is second place.

Comfort

My father is an imaginary slap on the wrist,
a frown through the telephone.

When he is home, we sit on his knee
at holiday parties only. The other men shift

their eyes and speak of youth like lost gold.
They all eat too much and retire to the TV

where they watch what stronger men do,
where they complain of what some man
won't let them do.

Us women and children accept this
like we don't sit in dark bedrooms alone, praying.

Amongst Children

I chase after. Squeal in delight because they run.
They're laughing so I laugh. The playground
is a wonder. I watch one after the other slide down
the yellow tube. The girl lets me play with her duckling.
I turn to Mama standing beneath the big tree. She nods.
The boy calls me to watch him climb wooden pieces
in the ground. Their parents yell, *Be careful.*
Every now and then their mama stares at me.
Ice cubes rattle in my tummy. Mama once told me
to trust my gut. The other mama stares at my mama, too.
They stare at each other until someone looks away.
The little girl asks why my hair stands like tree
branches instead of pointing down like hers. I shrug.

Bonnaroo, 2012

What is lonelier than truth: Finding yourself in a slow collapse one Tennessee day in June, standing in a circle of festival grins widening like taffy grossly stretched. On their cheeks unaffected by sweat, the crimson and black slashed paint, moist and heavy like gasoline-tinged pitchforks, leaps at you, their white teeth the glistening spark. Each girl's beaded fringe elongates around your neck and pulls, spanning colorblind millennia.

Ken, you think is his name, explains he mistook you for his girl Cathy, mistook the handful of your plump behind for her miniskirted savanna, your cropped curls for her dreads, mistook still as you yelped, his inked hand seizing more of you. And through it all his smile bulged against your back, the cruelty-free broad-spectrum limbs of his companions openly jiggling delight, your threatened tears sucked back in. These millennial yinzers clothed in images of D'Angelo and Prince, down for your culture, stoked the fire burning your sandals into ground, their blues and greens and browns clasping into Voltron.

Later you visualize knocking the teeth out of all their pasty mouths if only to convince yourself of divine restraint to explain why you let that obsequious grin slide down your face, telling each stranger you've forgiven this accidental fondle. It's like Desmond Tutu shaking de Klerk's hand 'cause if you offered less than exoneration, what would they think of you?

Girl Remembers a Place Even Columbus Cannot Miss

How curious the fear of sitting on the toilet
lest the worst kind of germ
climb upon my legs then spiral
deep within my bones.

The feeling resurfaces as I listen
to a mother and child at the public sink,
I lumbering above the danger in my stall.

I know its origin—the tense aura
of my mother demanding I not even think
about it as I fidget above the beasts,
scared my balance would give.

I hear her tell the boy to wipe his wet hands
on her pant leg because the hand dryer
transforms into a roaring lizard when it's on.

I wish mine remembered how it felt
to be five, to see the world as something
she could stop from swallowing me—

how her voice could have eaten the monsters.
How the softness is what I'd recall.

Star-Crossed East to West

We weep for ourselves on cue.
Eye the other for apologies then together,
sweep the broken glass and make plans
to redecorate our shame—no more
letting anger plaque between our seams.
You won't ask why I translate every name
you call me into a hard-earned reverie.
I won't ask how you can worship Black women
then tell me I am everything but one.

American Archipelago

And the overwhelming majority—almost all—behaved just like that: without any spirit, helplessly, with a sense of doom.

—Aleksandr Solzhenitsyn
The Gulag Archipelago

Lynne Isbell says snakes exist to sharpen our sight
so we can see them and avoid, see them and kill,
an adversary teaching us triumph since their creator
trusted some of us would. Like any call to power,
some will fail so others won't. Some will be told
they are leeches. Some will believe they are touched
by God. Some will be snakes teaching leeches
and the marked to believe they are all the same.

When I nurture the notion that suffering
makes us good—when I read the story that says
those with darker skin are less, tongues slither close.

Dream Dialogue Where My Mother Talks to the Photograph of Her and Her Parents Smiling, 1984

Mommy with your afro picked as halo
buckteeth framed by cigarette
telling me Daddy ain't this
whenever you're home and got a second
whenever I'm tending to your children

then Daddy with his afro sparse
as his yellow skin telling you you ain't this
when he's home and got a second
when you let him come home

my heart beating honor
this father honor this mother
though they don't know how to be
though neither can see how I clutch home
like it's a crumb buttered with grief

Dream Dialogue Where I Recount the Rape of My Father's Great Oma, 1896

He knocks on your door like an old friend
you know it's his slick knuckles
splintering your wood
soiling the same door Benji carried you
through days after being erected
by his own hands

You know he'll enter
put his fingers on your stomach
where Benji caressed before Margo's birth

Thank God
the children aren't home

You clench

A thousand suns etch into memory
cradling your eyes before he snaps your wrist

the dress of rough linen dyed blue
that Mama fixed to cinch your waist
Daddy's joy from every harvest sown and well reaped
a little boy shades brighter than the woman holding his hand

II

A Haunting

A sepia-tinged 1980 haunts every sleep that begins dull-dark,
my mother's mother locked behind her bedroom door. Every knock
from my mother's eight-year-old fist is met with audible sobs
immediately muffled. It is then her job to fix breakfast, to chop
the tomatoes plucked from Grandmother's garden.
Mother rouses the younger children from feigned sleep.
Grandfather still isn't home.

When she walks them to their classrooms at Weinland Park,
her siblings clutch at each hand like they think she will leave them.
My mother promises always to meet them at that part
of the wire fence that bends toward home, no matter how
they twist it. They relax; they know she keeps her promises.

Once home, music greets them from the kitchen.
Grandmother dances and whisks eggs. Bellows Temptations
and kisses all their heads. Sends Hazel to the garden and holds
Charlie's hand, her grin toothy, and between cigarette-tinged hums,
she asks about school, asks if my mother wants to help
knead dough for rigatoni. Charlie claps his hands.
He is young enough to still hope. When Grandmother flours
Mother's palms, she is gentle. Their hands are almost the same size,
she notes like Mother hasn't noticed. Nothing about this moment
changes what I know and when I wake, dry doppio zero cements
my palms around a tomato juice cache of sudden succor.

Memory of Star-Crossed Leaving Fingerprints

Sat on his floored mattress.
Wolfed down tiny pieces
of cheap clams billowing
in dark broth. The heat's off,
been off since before
you met him. This Columbus
winter demands excess warmth.
You move in to save him.
He doesn't shower daily,
you think, because it's cold.
You share cigarettes. Omit
the habits spring cannot thaw.

Variants of the Same Story, I

My father never said he loved my mother,
just that he wanted presence in my life.
My father, Black man in college,
neighborhoods away from that gang life,
never said he loved my mother
implying he'd put up with her bullshit
because she, too, was light
plus didn't I need his presence.
What if my mother was darker:
What if he loved her.

Serenaded by a Prince or Symbol

I beg the chlorine to disintegrate
my panic spasm crippled flesh
refused perfection.
Surrender swallows my mind;
perhaps Mama will chalk my angst
to irremediable defect.
Friends will remember the blonde
aesthetic I coveted, not the frizz,
the braces,
the dark mass I was.
Someone will send
Michael, whose skin
like pillow-fluff I wished
to rest upon, the love notes taped
to the back of my notebook.
Yes, this pulsing stretch of bubbles
will weigh me down to my Michael's
concrete kiss.
Except I'm lifted,
buoyed like a baby
into glittering sunlight,
left hacking pool water
from grave-robbed lungs.
On jagged stone I inhale
the sight of my lonesome brown hand
outstretched toward cirrus, beholden
to a future where I grow
from prepubescent
to something less than other.

Reminisce

Tell me again about that young Rhineland couple
you and Opa befriended on his tour overseas, how
you invited them to your home one Bangor summer.

Tell me how they marveled at the freshly painted
folk Victorian and how they slurped the crisp
watermelon fresh-picked in Columbus just for them,

the friends you wish to make feel at home
like they did for your young family in 1975.
Tell me about the bonfire, the sweet burn of tears

flicked away by the night as each adult laid bare
the same serenity interrupted by ego's empire, how all
at once the shadows and wind ceased their tricks.

Tell me how you found, that drizzling Sunday morning,
the wife naked in your kitchen boiling eggs for your boys
gaping in the breakfast nook. How your shriek

should've awakened Mount Hope's dead and how it sent
the spindly brunette up the stairs while you created
the tried-and-true tabula rasa defense all Negroes

have been spoon-fed, believing it to be the mush of God.

Like Crystal

Here amongst glittery crushed cans
and painted cigarette butts
someone mentions Stephen Miller.
In the single *New York Times* article
this Black girl browsed, he reminded her
of a high school crush, the balding
pale punk Guatemalan who said
she had nice feet after gifting him
a Howard Miller for his collection.

Her liberal friends smile as she prattles
admiration, calling his truculent
janitor critique a teenage quip,
his Machiavellian stance on immigration
conservative charm, concluding
the Duke three lucky someone
so reasonable came to their defense.
She knew girls like Crystal:
They deserved the pestilence of jail.

Fingerprints

Long ago, my father spent two Columbus winters
sans heat, the floor a symphony of dirt,
the whole place cigarette ash dusty.

Often on the mattress laid Julie, the barmaid
from Zeno's. She liked hearing him scold
White people then seeing where he lived and how.

She liked being told she had no soul
before their bodies convalesced beneath
the comforter, before she went home to her heat.

Yearn

Somewhere behind that lush
of chestnut hair and Pantera tee
lies a cloak made heavy.

Here I sit with wrists wide enough
to carry the hem. My skin, dark
golden iris, proves my saving grace.

Let me annihilate your sins
with love. Let us hold hands
and bask within the shuddered

stares of strangers. Behind
every Superman: The shadow
of a woman like me.

Like Pontius Pilate washing his hands

he washes himself of your stink
after discharging his seed on your back.
It trickles down your sanguine sheets
much like the bloated steam rises
from beneath your closed bathroom door.
Again you wonder why he never invites
you to shower. You tell yourself that one
of these evenings you'll step beneath
the balmy water and soap his already
White skin. You remind yourself that he
is in your bathroom. You remember the last
time you crept through the cracked door
and placed your copper hands on the plastic
between your bodies, his eyes glossy with
ichor when you pulled. It's better to tiptoe
around such a memory than look at it
for what it is so on the bed you stretch, his
remaining sweat your hydrating solace.

Postcolonial Triumph

I want to be White
meaning
I want to be human
meaning
I want to be free
meaning
I want to live

Response/Ability

Share the photo of Keisha with tire marks cascading her back.
Remember the protest last night, the hungry eyes.
Ask the masses where were you.
Ask them taste blood in exchange for God.
After the ashes settle on the campus rooftops
and the downtown glass is swept,
pay for Speedway Marlboro's.
Listen to birds chirp and avoid the eyes
of every child still young enough to grow.

Bust Yoke

Someone wants to say it, wants
to milk the proof from my veins,
moisturize my dark eyes with it
till it explodes from my skin.
Look at how they dance
within my aura, how they make
language from my foremother's rape
with spit that slithers off
their wagging tongues, these people
who once claimed they discovered
what I knew all along.

Every pronouncement that they
don't mean me when they speak
of any other is another instance
where they know I won't look close
enough to see their whetted teeth
tracing ovals around
my throat, four centuries
not long enough for me to grow.

In Solidarity with Fate

That so many women are choked sounds like a blessing
because then I am not alone.
Mine was cruel and drunk but sad.
I wanted to comfort him but what my mother taught me
about comfort can be found in my first abortion.
Nothing curdles soul like the feeling of one sucked up.
Smarter men say we are party to a cycle,
that something generational dictates my choices.
Braver men fess up to nothing.
This must be labor, thinking
the choker's decision divinely instilled.

Dream Dialogue Where My Grandmother Talks to Her Husband

I don't love you but
when I call you answer

All my knocks lead
to an opened door

When you hold
my baby she is yours

Most men don't like
used women

Something in you
accepts me regardless

Something in me trusts
that you'll never

spill my blood
that no matter

what animosity grows
between us you won't go

Something in you
smells like my father

I don't love you
but where else can I go

III

III

What Cannot Be Touched

Fingers crisscrossed over my eyes is ritual.
Sex and the City plays and I hear, pretend
I comprehend the highfalutin language
of real career women. Boar bristle yank
after yank, I listen and pretend
Mama encourages what she previously forbade,
for it is through the television that we bond.
She'd hold my hand and tell me how pretty my curls,
finger small sections, and, gently, brush.
She'd say my hair reminds her of her own
and of her mother's. I'd ask her what *sex* means
and she'd weave a tale of the warmth the sun gives
without expecting anything from us, though it is clear
we must care for what she nurtures. She'd tell me
how incredibly obscene these TV women are,
despite their earthly pedestal. But we don't talk.

Star-Crossed Caveat

You know dropping addictions ain't easy,
know my mind been plastered with the drug,
White Jesus a face I see in every boy
I long to wrap my arms around even when
your arms rest round my shoulders. You know
the feeling since you also spend late nights
dragging free from friends who know the game
better than us a Wonder Woman of your own.
You know we're mad, dripping in talk
we learned might save us if we believe
intention can turn our faults into stardust.

Where It May

As a boy, my father plucked flowers outside the library.
He didn't know what kind,
just that they were yellow like sunlight, with dark
middles like his iris, exuding the same
warmth. Where he's from no one taught
the names of plants growing on this land.
He never knew he, too, could claim this honeyed dirt
flowing in his gold-spun blood.
Where he's from, people lied. No one knew why
people feared skin like his, or so they say. No one
knew anything but shame flowering where it may.

When I Remember the Same Old

Because I watched you jam to James Brown
in rebellion of your parents
the way I blared The Clash
in rebellion of my Black,
I must believe redemption's for me, too,

must desire the perfumed arms
of my grandmother, her early morning hymns
the same ones her Baptist great-granddaddy learned
from his grandmother, though then the song
was closer to the kind that breaks possession,

like when you play in darkness
and wonder from whence came belonging,
and if you'll tire of the sweet mirage
surrounding my distorted voluptas.

Genealogy of Wounds

We live in cycles, don't we: Like each generation
of my family beating children with oak branches
as if those branches don't mimic our veins,
we embrace the cloudless brimming from coffins
as our own. I keep reading as if I'll find the origin
of disconnection in books about race, as if
I'll learn how to turn dust to switches I can
reconnect to home. Maybe there's an answer
in the root rot overlooked like a noose
I begged a lover untangle. Maybe I will read
that we rolled in the dandelions and climbed trees
that never hurt us, leaves fluttering like a blink
that cups the bitter tears asleep no longer.

Pulled Pork

In Killeen, Texas we eat at bars that serve flesh
holy men call sin with sips of cold Dos Equis
in between licked lips. Here I've solved
the equation: The more I flatter,
the longer you'll stay, so I plaster glory
on your shoulders, titillated because you,
outta them all, adore Zadie Smith and admit
Stevie Wonder brings you zen. And how you gush
over little colored me, ruffling
the picked curls you know I wear for you.

Never do I bring up all the Black men and women
dying across these streets; never do I mention
their children gunned down in Mickey Mouse beds.
Instead, I learn appreciation for your precious beer,
focus on your translucent green eyes, and gulp
down chip after chip of stringy meat that ferments
in my stomach, sucking in the bloat as if you won't notice.

A Writer Reads at the Library Downtown

To the crowded room, she speaks of a brother
broken by crack and the friend who sold it to him.
She says she wrote down their truth,
not knowing if anyone would care
that her brother died, and his friend lived.

Answers preach themselves in our applause,
though no one asks if we, too, are a monstrosity
God allowed us to regurgitate as human.

Someone in the crowd asks the writer about her writing process.
Another asks why she's writing a young adult superhero novel,
the protagonist, Black. No one asks if she thinks love can exist
in a state of stress. If she harbors resentment for her community
or her brother's friend. How she can speak to this mostly
White audience living in a city where Linden and the Hilltop
might become the next Olde Towne East,
another Bronx, another South Park.
No one asks what she thinks about the event following
her reading: A double feature of *Cinderella* and *Snow White.*

I am the only one who sits during her standing ovation,
wondering if this blatant showing of my monster
makes me any more different from the audience or less.

Where Are You, Jessica Dash?

Where are you
when I need
to vent the woes
of that which is male,
my pent-up agony
voracious specks
of burn.

Who else but you
can hop
into this fire
then help extinguish
the shared yearn
and after tears,
pull from
a manila folder
manifestations of our insides
so perfectly stanza'd
and drenched in home.

We'd map our north nodes
and predict our next poems,
measure the width
of our noses,
the brownness
of our skin,
compute their ratio
to see if we are part
of the divine.

Where are you when I need
holding

and someone to hold,
like sisters born
from the other's body,
like twins
separated by birth.

Trying Hard to Find the Answer

Blame White people. Blame ya single mama. Blame salt, fat, and sugar. Blame that elementary school back in Linden with the broken air conditioner. Blame 5G. Blame ya no good daddy. Blame every liquor store on the corner. Blame GMO corn. Blame the world for being born. Blame ya hair for being nappy. Blame Kendrick Lamar. Blame the gourmet burger joint now next to your dilapidated foreign. Blame ya fast-ass friends. Blame *Black-ish*. Blame infiltrated marches. Blame Martin Luther King, Jr. Blame fascists. Blame God. Blame the trash bursting out the alley. Blame melanin. Blame Anthropologie and their "Nicks" who can ball. Blame Snow White. Blame every bus ride to the fancy Easton mall. Blame Trump. Blame every second spent barred from peace. Blame White people. Blame the police.

Miscegenation

Tell me these White boys don't see
into the future like their mamas
who taught them how to grind
the right kind of me out of midnight
so that their sons and daughters
won't suffer the same muscle cramping
mixing void of mercurial technology,
their sisters and brothers basking
in the scent of our flesh, not quite
their own genetic concoction
but close enough that when
they sink their teeth into skin,
what bleeds out assures.

A Neighbor Tells What Happened to My Father's Aunt in Chillicothe, 1983

The remains were clean except for
the bullet holes. I'm not surprised
he burned down the house.
Almost broke his back, building
that thing. A home fit, he said,
for a good and honest wife.

Still, we suspected. She was nice
but never talked about her parents.
Claimed Italian heritage,
wore his grandmother's bonnets
when it rained. Mentioned a sister or two,
maybe a brother. Claimed they lost touch.

One day, her sister showed up,
hair stretched higher than
the tallest sycamore down
by the Scioto. Jim hid it well,
at first, but that's the sort of thing
that eats at an honest man.
It was good of him to spare us the blood.

Dream Dialogue Where I Talk to My Father Like I'm Honest

Why do my sins feel less monumental
while yours still gut my heart of its pumping
so much I can't even ask how I've wronged you
so much I can't even ask what unnailed your wrists
so much I can't even see you as a child
wailing for his father and denied
God's plan sputtering on the same wind
you rode your bike against
your voice louder than any explanation
in case his absence had nothing to do
with you

Fear Response to Reflection

The video shows Antoine of Willow Springs
shot in the back, the policeman
tall gorilla inflicting acquiescence.

The girl watching left Willow Springs
and dined at pale feet,
drank their blood,
licked their mercy.
Called it home.
These friends say
she must crucify her ego.
This isn't about color.

Waiting for all to intuit her terror
is like waiting for the clouds
to disperse from monolith to specks:
Gorillas, too, are God's children.

A Platter

Tell your mother to kiss my cheek
and praise my come up.
Watch as she gifts me her wedding dress

then listen when I tell you how she watched
me squeeze my Baartman hips within
the silk and tulle.

Let me carry my shame blunted
in orange juice and vodka
then serve me suburbia on a platter

and plant children in my womb,
seeds with strawberry blonde wisps
and skin like yellow snow.

Thought Experiment from the Vine

You take a daughter of Eshu and tie her wrist to Satan,
hands sticky with books grabbed from lending libraries
littered in their sweet suburb as if crafted sentences and stanzas
could save the slow ripping of their spines.
You let 'em walk past American foursquares and Dutch colonials,
let 'em dream of riverside picnics with other mothers and fathers
raising children also pulled out the womb instead of caught.
Once home, Satan reads to her the verses and paragraphs
proclaiming concrete walls atop poisoned dirt will outlive time.
In the evening, they'll drink wine with the neighbors
and she'll listen as the men declare themselves proud heirs
of the first god, Cronus, and she'll nod her head while
  the women sigh
how stable life is on this land now that the men accept them
as equal. She'll eye one woman's husband a little too long
and wonder if he'd also take her from behind.

The Inventor of Peanut Butter

What other spoonful of heaven
would I swirl with overnight oats
lumpy with milked walnuts;
what other bite
keeps my mouth chewing
the moment you open yours
with a tongue so steeped in bile,
I almost throw you away
like the chocolate chips
I forbid myself in theory.

Once, I heard Vanzant say
the more we love someone,
the more unlovable we become.

I inhale globs of my savior
and thank the inventor
for what he must've known
when he created such cream
of weeping hallelujah
as you, my love, excite
the prospect of my anger.

As If Still

I am not hunky-dory, splashed upon a hot sidewalk
next to you watching the sun spill its mercy on the horizon.
It is your horizon, this ivy-laced suburb
a portrait hanging free in your nostalgia.
You point here and there, your former home
a Hallmark greeting surrounded by avenues
and green spaces that remember your laughter,
that cradled the broken pride of your first car crash,
that watched you punch your brother then disappear
into its woods, mulberry potions laced with black willow leaves
a bit of solace. A prosperous childhood, I suppose, since despite
its hiccups and squabbles, you love your family and they love you.

It is no accident that my insides scream with every step,
that I jostle beneath the sun's rays and yearn to raise my fist in its
direction,
this same sun spilling upon my youth though I couldn't see it,
my nostalgia dreaming of salvation for my people,
of creating time machines for every generation as if different versions
of me could travel back to plantations and ghettos
and cold houses with bowls of mercy, as if the sun
spilled in me something that could save them.

When a White boy says he prefers

you natural he means that he's seen enough fraud blondes to last a galactic year so he'll let you have a piece of yourself even if you don't want it: that ain't nothing strong about a woman who can't stand the tug of her own tangles: that the way your flat-ironed tresses contrast against your sun-stroked skin like a well-placed spotlight is an affront to his mother he need not sustain: that your cream-splashed spirals are exotic enough to excuse your Willow Springs-reppin' roots: that it's easier to bemoan the hoodrats when you, his dark Athena, look almost like them, serving as his cocoon.

A Poem for a Daughter, for a Son

None of it was about you.
It may take years to understand
like it took me, grappling
with long-armed bandits
who know precisely where
to wrap around the body
and when. The ones
who weren't mothered
must have rocks in our milk,
arsenic film on our gums, and thus
breath that blights each kiss.
Some of us get lucky.
If I could've learned which one
I was before I knew about you,
the story I tell might not have changed.

IV

I Have a Photo of My Mother as a Child

She looks like my daughter, mouth agape
and eyes wide, as if she is asking
why adults have less bones than children.

She must be looking at my grandmother
taking the photo, asking her this question,
learning instead that she is not to ask

questions, not aloud and not to her,
my grandmother, who was once a child
asking herself why she lived in a world

that gives children cruel mothers.

Star-Crossed Without the Sugar

We fed each other to wolves,
spoon after spoon of hours spent
unloading the totality
of our perfumed mania
into the open hands of descendants
to the root cause of what hurt in me
which is what hurts in you
which their palms clenched
then stuffed into mouths
we knew deep down weren't kin.

Hood

We jut Ma'at into our daily bread.
Turn mud into pyramid bricks,
shadows mapping the heavens
though we rise above the stars.
Invent language harmonious
with all creation.
Fight wars because here,
we are human
but fight wars with a delicacy
that uplifts the circle of life.

Or at least, this is what we learn
when we study our history
beyond enslavement.
Or at least, this is what we say
in our attempt to understand

how you can call us thugs
when we had Kush,
or predators when we conceived
words for time, or squash our fingers
when we find the right ladder
and thrust our way out of these hoods
designed to foster generational
defeat of what might otherwise be
a revival of the very minds apt enough
to map Antarctica's islands first.

Dream Dialogue Where I Offer Black Beans to My Coworkers

after Sarah Kirsch

Afternoons you and him mention how much y'all hate beans
Afternoons you both talk to me and not the other two like me
Afternoons it occurs to me that too many
of us with too many of you is oil and water

Afternoons you and him joke that I eat black beans too often
Afternoons I boast about the extra squeeze of lime
Afternoons without you I am with the ones like me
who eat every bowl I serve like it is slow-brewed divinity

Afternoons with you and him I undress my oil
wash myself   sing a disgust like silence

First Run

It started the morning I squeezed a fat lime
into a jar of chia and honey,
squeezed until the citrus slipped

and I pinched my own thumb.
It felt like all my dreams of death,
like an omen imploring I reinvent myself

while I still had time.
Outside the window, specks of sky
bounced around ominous gray.

The wind shook trees I thought immovable.
Starting another day felt safe
but instead, I laced my shoes and bolted.

Every other second, I gulped air
and noticed branches shimmering
as if their new growth were a mirage.

When the wind came, I kept going
and thanked the black maples struggling
to shield my slow pace from its girth.

There were robins lilting a birdsong sweet
as morning, and all the baby crocus asked
if I knew how to listen for spring,

as if the right answer would bring February sun,
velvet rays I'd ask to chastise the wind
even though it now felt fine on my naked arms.

For Bodies to Whom I Owe My Life

oh my God do I still wonder about melanin
wonder 'bout it's real relationship to the sun
real casual in the beginning, common I'm sure,
beginning with blue water we can't drink with all its salt
can't drink away my wonder each time Mama says, go
wonder 'bout life's mysteries away from here
life's too painful to play with questions you know will
play with you the way each of us play dumb, though eventually
each of us must walk the gilded path to what is called home

The Blacker

Catch me fondling stray thoughts of justice, a place
where the ones who need the most get exactly that.
The color of our skin is no accident if you believe
in God. Do our souls contain the blueprint
of revolution eager to upend that which God made
permissible? And we all know change is a cloud
that can turn into a waterless wisp or omnipresent storm.
Go to any continent and tell me the blacker the berry,
the greater the nonexistence of the enemy's sword.
Tell me every -ism doesn't start with the width of one's
nose. Tell me there must be a victim for every victor
and that war waged against the welcoming
is a war with the most delicious blood.

They Used to Chop Off the Penis

Progress says you can ask the police officer
if he is telling the truth and study
what crime does to a man after long enough.

Countless videos prove what happens
if you grow up believing the worst.

What evidence says our roots don't differ?
Each seedling sprouts a body, a tool
unfurling how many ways origin can be skinned.

When I Think About Malcolm X

He is feeling what I feel
when my neighbor asks me
what to tell his little niece
the first time
she is told she is prettier
than her dark mother,
like I'm someone worthy of trust,
maybe even kissed by God,
and here is how I can repay
such mercy.

The Guts That Come with Love

Zip-tied to the fence
across the street
from a dilapidated building
next to this high rise
in another revitalized downtown:
The faces of but fifty or so
Black people murdered
in the last five years
in this city alone.
The residents call it art,
the activists, a public announcement,
absolutely no one: A reminder
of what resources Black people have
to fix anything
                    (can't even fix themselves)

and what resources White people have
to fix anything
                    (can't even fix themselves).

And Transmuted

I am a woman.
I am not built to carry
a man
on my back.

Power
does not mean
all-being
all-doing.

Whatever I was allowed
I took
and transmuted.

I gave you
—a man—
my power
hoping
you would eat it
and transmute.

Death takes us all
and most
are not brave
about it.

This, I learned
from you.

Initiation

Waves smash all doubt I've failed.
At the edge, I bathe the parts of me
still hard to stomach. Salt wounds
my lips like too much honey, makes
them shine brighter than cratered moon.
My back sinks into wet shore, marking
me for trauma I no longer say I am.
These waters have always been
home. If I squash my toes into sand,
bury the hurt bits like lingering crumbs
swept into mother's palm and carried,
what can I build from the sown?

Intersectional Guillotine

Sweeping grand statements aren't enough—
if I asked for this, I've forgotten—
I don't look like my great-great-grandmother—
raped by a White man whose name I'll never know—
what did he annihilate that shimmers in my blood—
our incomplete erroneous memory writes history—
what of mine, when I ask how I've wronged you—
do I consider the oppression I might carry—
do I wear it like the earth upon Atlas—
what must I ask you to consider, if I haven't—
what is my art if not the question—
what is my responsibility—
what is yours—

Cento Across the Mutual Landscape

I will throw this bridge across
all feeling, like nothing in your world.

But to make something with those wounds,
knowing the knot of death, emphasizes

that cold, and you know it.
Not unlike those notes the horn would say

leftover talk in your head
and arrange them as fruit.

Whenever I move I go toward Home,
from a table already wet with His judgment

and with Etheridge one night reading the poem
"Ilu, the Talking Drum,"

the last guitar line
breath, the drifter's home.

Dream of Clintonville After We All Move In

> *You and we are different races. We have between us a broader difference than exists between almost any other two races. Whether it is right or wrong I need not discuss, but this physical difference is a great disadvantage to us both, as I think your race suffer very greatly, many of them by living among us, while ours suffer from your presence. In a word we suffer on each side.*
>
> —Abraham Lincoln
> *Address on Colonization to a Deputation of Negroes*

We still in this country and, yes, this city-center now ours. We ain't gotta tell how, don't need to write no treatise when our hips and twists tell the story just as well. Like tree after tree wind swished, we bloom, breathing early amens encased in spring sun, and learn even quiet can be a blessing. We finally acquired the taste of our masters, Robinson and Kamau saluting our prayer line, mouths open for morsels Chappelle and Morrison feed. The child in us makes peace with an ancestor, who knew the soil where a body spills seed and blood is home

and on these porches like a well-timed psalm, we watch our children swirl amongst the mallows and carpenter bees, amongst the creeping thyme and yarrow, amongst the slick sharp grass and hippy Oshun statues and endless dominoes and hieroglyphic candles and smoked meat laughter where many of us gather, two-steppin' outside libraries brimming with Dogon and Malinke and Baule while every old Chevy thumps the heavy nectar of our rap. Even the birds hear, their calling songs homophonic with our modern Ma'at

that every child knows like the name of at least one star, like every house with a lawn once held a Black Lives Matter sign

been deemed historic. Fathers and mothers help bury love notes and telescopes we want our descendants digging up. The streets are not littered with bones and our recluses, who remember what came before, leave their homes at least once, allowing a child to lead them through a ravine so baffling with joy. *Nothing's special about us,* they lament. *God gave us a challenge our hands could whet.*

Food That Was Cheap

They get it. Hundreds of years later,
we struggle still. They act like
they can't comprehend
ancestral savageness,
the epigenetics of it all.

They want us to keep telling
stories of neighbors
selling crack by the school
of our mother's beatings
our brother's rape
our father's absence
our sister's overdose—
the specifics icing
between layers they know
they baked.
They know we'll paint
write
sing
dance
act
out the misery
without a dagger their way.

They'll throw us all the change
our cupped palms can hold.
They'll let us sweat on their good sheets
and even tell us how great their sacrifice
must be, to hunger for us.

When You Hear Love Talkin'

I live amongst the Negroes
who don't value old grammar rules
who break glass upon the sidewalk
each shard a sharp point
with which to cut their lips
I live here watching
our children devour
every brownie I bake for them
between the thumping bass of feet
between each house and moonlit street
between the cheap gin and tonics I down
as if a buzzed stupor
will loosen my own strict tongue
will guide me toward
the right semantics
with which to bandage
their broken hearts
with which to tell them
a mouth leaking crystals
is all I got to give

What the Star-Crossed Notice

Last May's new moon was different. Up late,
we each nursed seeds inherited from our mothers,
cracked and shriveled and gray though we knew
we'd douse the shit in gravy, still eat the growth.

In hindsight, I knew better, had once spent noons
watching robins nestle lush oak, had grown
the courage to question why no one who looked
like me shared tales of babes beneath turquoise eggs

kept warm by a mother, their father perched
on the neighbor's gutter watching as the storyteller
lit cigarettes and poured Apothic Red into everyone's jar,

life rituals in a world hell-bent on pouring gravy
on our seeds so when the hybrids reached our palms,
we wouldn't hesitate to eat.

Blessing the Breakup

after Lucille Clifton

may the border
that existed already
like a coffee stain in your favorite white mug
give us wind
beyond what waves
transmit from Yemoja's moon
may we remember
our borrowed breath
so certain it knew
its enemy   so certain
a dirty room could be smudged
of sin us humans shoulder bounce

Star-Crossed Daughter at 23 Months

Within porcelain, you splash away
the summer's cantaloupe juice
and dirt, me and Daddy beaming over
you like eclipsed sun. We soak
up one another's sweat. Synergetic
cords holding together our limbs,
our cells shiver, enticed by bountiful
joy circling this matchbox space.
When your father sits, I yank
out those cords battered by my post
traumatic baby's breath goading him
with passive curses and he rubs
my legs with mercy, us clairvoyantly
sharing the brunt of my shame.
Olive water drips from your sparse
coiled hair. You stand surefooted and
pour this same ale out an apple-adorned
bucket, soaking our feet to bone.

Man Dressed Daughter at 23 Months

Notes

"Cento Across the Mutual Landscape" consists of lines from the following poems from Christopher Gilbert's collection, *Across the Mutual Landscape*:

"And, Yes, Those Spiritual Matters"
"Beginning by Destruction"
"Beginning by Example"
"Beginning by Value"
"Chosen to Be Water"
"The Directions"
"Enclosure"
"Glimpses of Power"
"Horizontal Cosmology"
"Muriel Rukeyser as Energy"
"Speaking Things"
"This Bridge Across"

Acknowledgments

Grateful acknowledgment is made to the following publications in which these poems first appeared, sometimes in earlier versions:

African American Review: "Amongst Children," "Food That Was Cheap," and "Star-Crossed Daughter at 23 Months"
The Cape Rock: "The Inventor of Peanut Butter"
Cordella: "Intersectional Guillotine"
Duende: "Pulled Pork"
Glass: A Journal of Poetry: "Bust Yoke"
Heavy Feather Review: "The Blacker"
Hobart: "Hood," "Initiation," and "Where Are You, Jessica Dash?"
Kissing Dynamite: "As If Still" and "Where It May"
Matter Monthly: "Like Crystal"
Mom Egg Review: "What Cannot Be Touched"
Obsidian: "Bonnaroo, 2012," "Girl Remembers a Place Even Columbus Cannot Miss," "Miscegenation," and "Reminisce"
Spoken Black Girl: "I Have a Photo of My Mother as a Child"
Transition: "Bravata"
Writers Resist: "Response/Ability"
Zone 3: "Serenaded by a Prince or Symbol"

"The Guts That Come with Love" was published in *Metamorphosis: An Anthology* (Ohio Writers' Group, 2022).
"Yearn" was published in *PUNK: An Anthology of Poetry*, edited by Christine Taylor (Kissing Dynamite, 2022).

Thank you to everyone who helped bring this work to life: the CavanKerry Press team, Momo Alvarado, Joy Arbor, Natasha Kane, Trevor Ketner, Marcus Jackson, Kathy Fagan Grandinetti, Allison Pitinii Davis, Karen Scott, Miccau McClelland, Leslie Battle, Marquita Byars, Rachael Scott, Sayuri Ayers, Scott Woods, Tiffany Lawson,

Renia White, Arah Ko, my literary and artistic muses, and all those unnamed 'cause I unintentionally forgot but you know you contributed. I give thanks.

Risë—Piece of my heart, my gut, my soul. When the student is ready, the teacher appears. May this publication honor you the way you have honored me.

Akhim—I am a better woman, a better writer, and a mother because of you. Thank you.

Akhilah—What a blessing, what a treasure, you are. You and God saw fit to make me your mother. There is no greater honor. I love you, bruh sister Kiki.

All fifty eleven of my parents—I exist because of all of you, which means I come from the best.

To my ancestors—Here is another offering. Thank you for your help, your guidance, your jokes, your whispers. Let's make the next one a lil' more grand, okay?

To anyone who's ever given me a lesson—Your presence is not unnoticed. How could it be? You are another bit of life, like me, in the grand scheme of eternity. I give thanks.

CavanKerry's Mission

A not-for-profit literary press serving art and community, CavanKerry is committed to expanding the reach of poetry and other fine literature to a general readership by publishing works that explore the emotional and psychological landscapes of everyday life, and to bringing that art to the underserved where they live, work, and receive services.

Other Books in the Emerging Voices Series

Orange, Noel Quiñones
Girl Trouble, Diana Whitney
Singing from the Deep End, Rebecca Hart Olander
The Last Beast We Revel In, Noah Davis
Beyond the Watershed, Nadia Alexis
In Inheritance of Drowning, Dorsía Smith Silva
Seraphim, Angelique Zobitz
When Did We Stop Being Cute?, Martin Wiley
Boy, Tracy Youngblom
In the River of Songs, Susan Jackson
Mausoleum of Flowers, Daniel B. Summerhill
A Half-Life, David S. Cho
Uncertain Acrobats, Rebecca Hart Olander
Her Kind, Cindy Veach
Deke Dangle Dive, Gibson Fay-LeBlanc
Pelted by Flowers, Kali Lightfoot
Rise Wildly, Tina Kelley
Set in Stone, Kevin Carey
Scraping Away, Fred Shaw
Rewilding, January Gill O'Neil
My Oceanography, Harriet Levin
See the Wolf, Sarah Sousa
Gloved Against Blood, Cindy Veach
Threshold, Joseph O. Legaspi
Jesus Was a Homeboy, Kevin Carey
Eating Moors and Christians, Sandra M. Castillo
Esther, Pam Bernard
Love's Labors, Brent Newsom
Places I Was Dreaming, Loren Graham

Misery Islands, January Gill O'Neil
Spooky Action at a Distance, Howard Levy
door of thin skins, Shira Dentz
Where the Dead Are, Wanda S. Praisner
Darkening the Grass, Michael Miller
The One Fifteen to Penn Station, Kevin Carey
My Painted Warriors, Peggy Penn
Neighborhood Register, Marcus Jackson
Night Sessions, David S. Cho
Underlife, January Gill O'Neil
The Second Night of the Spirit, Bhisham Bherwani
The Red Canoe: Love In Its Making, Joan Cusack Handler
WE AREN'T WHO WE ARE and this world isn't either, Christine Korfhage
Imago, Joseph O. Legaspi
Through a Gate of Trees, Susan Jackson
Against Which, Ross Gay
The Silence of Men, Richard Jeffrey Newman
The Disheveled Bed, Andrea Carter Brown
The Fork Without Hunger, Laurie Lamon
The Singers I Prefer, Christian Barter
Momentum, Catherine Doty
An Imperfect Lover, Georgianna Orsini
Soft Box, Celia Bland
Rattle, Eloise Bruce
Eyelevel: Fifty Histories, Christopher Matthews
GlOrious, Joan Cusack Handler
The Palace of Ashes, Sherry Fairchok
Silk Elegy, Sondra Gash
So Close, Peggy Penn
Kazimierz Square, Karen Chase
A Day This Lit, Howard Levy

This book was printed on paper from responsible sources.
The text of *Phantom Hue* was set in Arno Pro.